AMAZING GOODNESS

*31 Days to
a Revelation of
the Goodness of God*

BY SAMUEL MARTINEZ

All scripture quotations, unless otherwise noted, are from the *New King James Version*. Copyright © 1982 by Thomas Nelson Inc. Used by Permission. All rights reserved.

Scripture quotations taken from the *Amplified Bible*. Copyright © 1954, 1958, 1962, 1964, 1965, 1987 By the Lockman Foundation. Used by permission. (www.Lockman.org)

Copyright © 2015 Samuel Martinez

Amazing Love Ministries
216 S. Citrus St. P.O. BOX 503
West Covina Calif. 91791

Bush Publishing & Associates books may be ordered at www.BushPublishing.com or www.Amazon.com.
For further information, please contact:
Bush Publishing & Associates
www.BushPublishing.com

ISBN-13: 978-1-944566-01-2

All rights reserved. No part of this book shall be reproduced, stored in a retrieval system, or transmitted by any means, electronic, mechanical, photocopying, recording, or otherwise, without written permission from the publisher.

Dedication

To our Lord and Savior THE manifestation of the goodness of God, the Father.

To every minister of the Gospel who has taught me something about the goodness of God. They are too numerous to note them all in this page. I will mention a few, however. Kenneth Copeland, Creflo Dollar and Joseph Prince. I give a great thanks to them.

To my wonderful wife—how well I remember that day in 69! She has been the greatest expression of the goodness of God in my life, other than Jesus.

To my son Andrés Clemente Martinez the second greatest expression of the goodness of God in my life, and to his wife, Tanya, my daughter-in-law, who has shown me nothing but the goodness of God since she married my son.

To Helen McLeod who tirelessly proofread this manuscript.

*Oh, give thanks
to the Lord
for He is good!
Because His mercy
endures forever*

Table of Contents

Introduction		7
1	The Lord Is Good and His Mercy Endures Forever	9
2	Our Absolute God Who Is Absolute Good	11
3	Do Not Even Think About It	13
4	A Good God Gives Good Things	15
5	God of the Much More	17
6	Expect to See	19
7	Mercy Is Good	21
8	Healing Is Good	23
8	Divine Protection Is Good	25
10	Prosperity Is Good	27
11	Abundance Is Good	31
12	Marriage Is Good	33
13	Full of Compassion	35
14	The Lord Is Good to All	37
15	The God of Restoration, Part One	39

16	The God of Restoration, Part Two	41
17	Taste and See	45
18	His Goodness Leads to Repentance	47
19	The Good Shepherd	51
20	The Gospel	53
21	God the Great	55
22	Releasing His Goodness in Our Lives, Part One	57
23	Releasing His Goodness in Our Lives, Part Two	61
24	A Year Crowned with Goodness	65
25	The Crown of Goodness	67
26	Goodness and Mercy Are Following Me	69
27	In the Beginning, Good	71
28	His Glory	73
29	The Good Hand of the Lord	75
30	Filled With All Goodness	77
31	Show and Tell	79

Epilogue: Receive Him Who Is Goodness—
   Come on Home 81

Verses on the Goodness of God 83

Appendix 85

About the Author 89

Amazing
The Goodness
of God

Introduction

God, the true God, the God of Abraham, Isaac and Jacob is good. The God and Father of our Lord Jesus Christ is good. You need to get a revelation of this my friend. Read one chapter a day slowly and take time to grasp the truths in this book. He loves you and because He loves you the outflow of His love is that He desires to do you good.

Acts 10:38 states that God anointed Jesus of Nazareth and that He went about doing good. All that Jesus did while on the earth was good because He only did what He saw His father do which was and will always be good.

A book on the goodness of God is a book on God Himself since He is All good and All loving. Let this book change the way you think. This book is not intended to be read in one sitting although it can be. If you do read it in one day take time to go through it again one chapter per day slowly. Take time to do the confessions. When you go through this book completely take time to read it again for another 31 days. Make it a lifetime endeavor to know more and more of the love of God. We will spend all eternity studying His goodness and seeing it in action. He is truly good. No one book can contain everything on the goodness of God.

I pray for you as you start to read this book. Father, strengthen my readers with might by Your Spirit in their inner man. I pray that Christ may dwell in their hearts by faith and being rooted and grounded in love may be able to comprehend the breadth, length, depth and height and to know the love of Christ that passes mere human knowledge that they may be filled with all the fullness of God, in Jesus' name.

Now enter with expectancy that as you read and receive your life will never be the same. May the phrase God is good become more than just a nice Christian saying for you. Be Blessed as you spend time in this book.

31 DAYS TO

A REVELATION OF

THE GOODNESS OF GOD

1

THE LORD IS GOOD AND HIS MERCY ENDURES FOREVER

Psalm 118:1, Oh, give thanks to the Lord, for He is good! For His mercy endures forever.

This is one of the greatest verses in the entire Bible. These four words (the Lord is good) describe the total essence of who God is. Hebrews 11:6 states that he who comes to God must believe that God is. Not that He exists, although many translations render this verse in that manner, but that He IS. The word 'IS' refers to the truth that God never changes. When the Bible describes God as the One Who was and is and is to come, it means God is and will always be the same.

God was, is, and will forever be good. To say things such as He used to heal and do mighty works but that He no longer does, is to deny that God IS. The Lord IS good refers to His nature but it also points to the truth that God is anything and everything good you need Him to be. Absolute good. Extremely good. All good. There is no bad in Him. Nothing in the Bible or in Christianity can be understood without this understanding. It is no coincidence that everything God created in Genesis chapter 1 was called good because the very first thing God wants you to know about Him is that He is good. Receive this in your heart and say it with your mouth. The Lord, my God, is good and His mercy endures forever. We serve a good God!

....

Confession

My Father is good to me and His mercy endures forever.

....

2

OUR ABSOLUTE GOD
WHO IS ABSOLUTE GOOD

James 1:17, Every good gift and every perfect gift is from above, and comes down from the Father of lights, with Whom there is no variation or shadow of turning.

It was Kenneth Copeland who first introduced me to the absolute nature of God. He mentions in one of his teachings about absolute cold. This is a foreign concept to most people. It was to me until I heard him talk about it.

Even when it is 50 degrees below zero outside the cold air still has some heat in it. This sounds strange to me. For cold to be **absolute cold** the temperature would have to be around 450 degrees below zero, Fahrenheit. That would be cold with absolutely no heat in it.

In the same way God is absolute good. There is no bad or evil in Him. None whatsoever. That is why James

1:17 states that every good and perfect gift is from above. Only that which is good is perfect and comes from Him. Perfect can be likened to absolute. God never changes. He is and will always be good. James further brings out that there is no shadow of turning in God. In other words, don't even <u>think</u> about Him changing. Absolute good means we should not even think about God being behind a loved one's death or the author of some calamity. He is and will always be good. If it is good it is from God. If it is bad or evil it is from satan.[1]

In 1 John 1:2 the Apostle John states that <u>the</u> life was manifested. God is absolute life. Since God has no shadow of turning then He is absolute light. Since He IS love (not have love but IS love) then He is absolute love. Since every good and perfect gift comes from Him then He is absolute good. This is our absolute God. Absolute good, absolute life, absolute light and absolute love.

· ·

Confession

God is absolutely good to me. He has always been and will always be good to me.

· ·

---

1 John 10:10

3

Do Not Even Think About It

2 Corinthians 10:5… Bringing every thought into captivity to the obedience of Christ,…

At my local Christian Television station some parking spots are marked by a sign that reads, "Do not even think about parking here." James 1:17 (chapter two) seems to say, "Do not even think about God not being or wanting to be good to you." Do not even think about parking your mind there. Since God is Absolute good He will not use calamity to teach us. God uses His Word[1] and His Holy Spirit[2] to teach us. The Bible even uses the word good to refer to the Bible—God's GOOD Word.[3]

Psalm 143:10 states that God's Spirit is good. God uses His Spirit and goodness to teach us and guide us to all things that are good and to all truth. Reject every

---

1 2 Timothy 3:16
2 John 16:13
3 Hebrews 6:5

thought that God was behind something evil that came into your life. Do not even allow the deception that God did not cause it but allowed it for some strange purpose. This can be even worse. In other words, He could have stopped it but stood by. Many times it is our own actions and decisions that bring negative things into our lives but even there His goodness and grace are available to help us. James 1:5 shows that God is there to give us wisdom in the trials of life and will not refuse our request for help. The Amplified Bible indicates that He will give wisdom without reproaching or faultfinding.

When we refuse to entertain the thoughts of satan that God was in any way behind a calamity, He can now teach us by His good Spirit and Word how to overcome in any negative situation. This, my friend, is the goodness of God. By His good Spirit He leads me into the land of uprightness.[4] Believe and receive this.

••

Confession

I declare my mind free from all thoughts
contrary to the goodness of God.
I will not park my mind there.

••

---

4 Psalm 143:10 Amplified Version

4

A Good God Gives Good Things

Matthew 7:11, If you then, being evil (natural) know how to give good gifts to your children, how much more will your Father Who is in heaven give good things to those who ask Him.

John 9:3,4, Jesus answered, "Neither this man nor his parents sinned, but that the works of God should be revealed in him. I must work the works of Him who sent Me while it is day; the night is coming when no one can work."

Most people assume this passage points to God making the man blind to be able to heal him later and get glory from his healing. But let's use our heads for one minute. With so many blind people around why did God have to make ONE more sick to heal him later? Secondly, would you do this to your own son? Of course not. If we being natural parents know how to give good things to our children how MUCH MORE will God give good things to us.

Going back to John chapter 9, since the Greek had no punctuation, eliminating the period at the end of verse three of the 9th chapter would point to the truth that the "works of Him that sent me" was not referring to the <u>blindness</u> but to the man being <u>healed</u>. In other words, the works of Him who sent Jesus (the Father God) is not making people sick but making people well.

Jesus Himself taught us to pray God's will be done on earth as it is in heaven. There is no sickness in heaven. This man was healed because healing is the "works of Him that sent me." Even a person dogmatic of the King James punctuation has to see that Jesus stated, "I must work the works of Him who sent me" and then healed the man. **Healing** is the work of God not sickness. Our Father is good and there is no shadow of turning in Him. He only gives good things.

· ·

Confession

I praise You Father that You are a good
God who gives good things. Therefore, good
things are coming to me today!

· ·

5

GOD OF THE MUCH MORE

Romans 5:17, For if by one man's offense death reigned through the one, MUCH MORE those which receive abundance of grace and of the gift of righteousness will reign...

Luke 12:28, If then God so clothes the grass...how MUCH MORE will He clothe you, O you of little faith?

Returning to Matthew 7:11 we find Jesus stating that if we as natural parents <u>know</u> how to give good things to our children then how MUCH MORE God wants to give to us. Now get this revelation. Because God is absolute good and <u>knows</u> more than we do He wants to do MUCH MORE for us.

In Romans 5:8-9 Paul points to the MUCH MORE nature of God by showing us that He loved us and died for us while we were sinners BUT wants (now that we are His children) to do MUCH MORE for us. Wait! Much more then dying for us? The point Paul is making is that God's goodness never peaks. Now that we are His children He wants to and can now do even much more for us. This is what eternity with God will be like. God showing us His MUCH MORE for all time. We see in Ephesians 2:4-7 that in eternity God will show us the exceeding riches of His kindness. Not just His kindness but the <u>exceeding</u> riches of His kindness. Our God is the God of the MUCH MORE. He is MUCH MORE good that we can ever ask or think.[1]

When we have been in heaven ten thousand years (yes I know eternity has no time) and think we have seen all the goodness of God, He will show us another whole level of His goodness. In other words, He will show us much more than what He had shown us up to that time. He is truly good! Eternity will simply be God showing us much more upon much more upon much more of His goodness.

······································

Confession

I thank You Father that You are the God of the MUCH MORE. Therefore, I expect MUCH MORE good to come to me today.

······································

---

[1] Ephesians 3:20

6

EXPECT TO SEE

Psalm 27:13, I would have lost heart, unless I had believed that I would see the goodness of the Lord In the land of the living.

Psalm 27:14, Wait on the Lord; Be of good courage, And He shall strengthen your heart;

My friend, Bible hope is expectation. Someone said that expectation is the breeding ground for miracles. Do you get up in the morning expecting to see the goodness of the Lord? Well, you should or as noted above you will lose heart. In John chapter 11 Jesus told Martha, the sister of Lazarus who had just died, that if she believed she would see the glory of God. In a coming chapter we will see that one of the manifestations of the glory of God is His goodness. God wants us to believe in His goodness so that we will be expecting to see it in our lives every day.

David concludes the 27th Psalm by encouraging us to wait on the Lord and be of good courage. Friend, be of good courage. Believe that He is good and that He loves you and God will strengthen your heart as David adds as he finishes the Psalm.

In the next few chapters you will have an opportunity to read about some of the good things that God has given us. Healing is one of them along with divine protection, prosperity and marriage. God does not want His people destroyed due to a lack of knowledge. God is good and everything that comes from Him is good. Even what He commands us to do is for our good.[1] Live in expectation today of seeing His goodness every day. Expect to see. This is His will for you because He is good.

....

CONFESSION

I live in continual expectation of seeing
the goodness of God in my life
because He is good.

....

---

1 Deuteronomy 10:13

7

MERCY IS GOOD

Psalm 109:21…Because Your mercy is good, deliver me.

The Lord is good and His mercy endures forever. Let's key in on the word AND. It is a conjunction that makes the statements before and after it on the same plane or level. The Lord is good, as we have already seen, AND His mercy endures. This means that mercy is good. Simple isn't it? However, most people do not seem to get this. Some have defined mercy as <u>not getting what we deserve</u> (such as hell) but that is only half of the definition. Yes, we did not get hell but in our day to day life so much good comes that we did not deserve.

In fact, everything that God has given us has been undeserved. We did not deserve Jesus coming to take our place and deliver us. However, He came and favored us because of His grace. We could say that His mercy saved us, delivered us.

According to the above verse, mercy is the delivering power of God. Because He is merciful He will deliver us. Do you recall Psalm 91:14 where the psalmist states by the Holy Spirit that God will deliver us as we set our love upon Him? Setting our love upon Him means that we love Him but that we first of all believe that He loves us. How can we love Him without first believing that He loves us?

At times we make bad choices that get us in hot water. We beat ourselves up and actually cut ourselves off from His mercy and grace. Somehow we feel that we got ourselves into the mess so we have to get ourselves out. But think of this. The greatest mess we were ever in was when we needed a Savior. There was nothing we could do to save ourselves from sin and hell so we relied on His mercy and grace and He delivered us. Thank Him for His mercy, for His delivering power. His mercy is there to deliver you from any situation. In His mercy He will instruct you and direct you to victory. Mercy is good.

Confession

The Lord's mercy endures forever toward me.
He will deliver me!

8

HEALING IS GOOD

Acts 10:38, "how God anointed Jesus of Nazareth with the Holy Spirit and with power, Who went about doing GOOD and HEALING all who were oppressed by the devil, for God was with Him.

Acts 4:9, "If we this day are judged for a GOOD deed done to a helpless man, by what means he has been MADE WELL,

Luke 6:9, Then Jesus said to them, "I will ask you one thing: Is it lawful on the Sabbath to do GOOD or to do evil, to SAVE LIFE or to destroy?"

The word AND in Acts 10:38 shows us that healing is definitely good. Of course, this makes sickness bad. I am not saying that a person who is sick is bad only that we should not be confused in calling sickness good and healing evil. In Luke chapter 6 we have the story of the man healed on the Sabbath day. When Jesus was questioned about healing on the Sabbath He defended His action by calling healing good. In chapter four of the book of Acts, the apostles when questioned by the religious leaders about the healing of a man born lame, called healing good.

God wants ALL His children well. Psalm 107:20 states that God sent His word and healed them. In the next verse the psalmist adds, "Oh, that men would praise the Lord for His goodness…." Yes, healing is the goodness of God. Note how many people in asking Jesus for healing cried out for mercy.[1] Healing is good as mercy is good. Believe that God wants you well. Read 1 Peter 2:24 and Psalm 103:3. Begin to declare that by the stripes of Jesus you are, present tense, healed. He wants you well. Believe in His goodness. Healing is good. Healing is the goodness of God in action.

···

Confession

I receive my healing today because my Father is good and wants me well. By the stripes of Jesus I am healed.

···

---

1 (Matthew 9:27, Matthew 15:22, Matthew 17:15, Mark 10:47, Luke 17:13)

9

DIVINE PROTECTION IS GOOD

Psalm 91:14-16, Because he has set his love upon Me, therefore I will deliver him; I will set him on high because he has known My name. He shall call upon Me, and I will answer him; I will be with him in trouble; I will deliver him and honor him. With long life I will satisfy him, and show him My salvation."

Psalm 91:10, No evil shall befall you, Nor shall any plague come near your dwelling;

There are so many promises in the Bible for divine protection but the above are some of the best. Do you love the Lord? I believe you do since you are reading this book. It is encouraging that all God desires from us to protect us is to love Him. Not hard at all when you have a revelation of His goodness. With long life I will satisfy him. God does not want our life cut short. His plan is for us to live long and live strong. He desires us to live as long as it takes to satisfy us and as long as it takes us to fulfill the calling on our lives. It is a lie of the devil to state that, "when your number is up, your number is up and you die."

Psalm 91:1 starts with the mention of the place of His Divine protection—the secret place of the Most High God. What is that secret place? It is a revelation of His great love and a revelation of His great goodness. It is practicing His presence by constantly meditating on His great love for us.

In the new covenant we are present tense in the secret place of the Almighty. In John 1:18 the Bible teaches us that Jesus is in the bosom of the Father. Since I am one with Him I can also state that I am also in the bosom of the Father.

Now add to these truths your confession of faith in Psalm 91:2. Say of the Lord that He is your refuge, your fortress, your God and that in Him you trust. Yes, the Lord is good and His mercy endures forever. Divine protection is good.

....

Confession

I abide in the secret place of the Most High God because God is my Father and He loves me. I am in His bosom, therefore, no evil befalls me and no plague comes near me.

....

10

PROSPERITY IS GOOD

Jeremiah 33:9, Then…all nations of the earth…shall fear and tremble for all the goodness and all the prosperity that I provide for it.

In the above verse God's goodness and prosperity are tied together. God is not against us having money only not letting money have us. It is interesting that the word of God calls such things as houses, furniture and other things "goods." In Deut. 28:11 God stated that He wants us to be blessed with goods and makes it clear that He is talking about material things. In the old covenant obedience was the condition for material blessings. In the new covenant they were given to us when we were born-again.[1] We obey out of the recognition of His great love and goodness.

If you make a study of the word <u>good</u> in the Old Testament you cannot but fall in love with the God of the

---

1 Romans 8:32, Ephesians 1:3, 2 Peter 1:3

Bible. The word good in the Hebrew carries the idea of prosperity. I wonder why it has been so hard for us to reconcile in our minds that prosperity is one of the blessings of a good God. In the New Testament the word saved includes the thought of wholeness. Wholeness includes material well being.

When the rich young ruler came asking what he had to do to inherit eternal life,[2] Jesus told him to go sell, give and to follow Him. He was not addressing riches as bad. He was trying to get the young man off his dependence on his own efforts to prosper and getting him to prosper by his dependence on the Lord God, Jehovah. The young man was actually coming to Jesus bragging on his works of righteousness. This young Jewish man had forgotten Proverbs 10:22 that the blessing of the Lord IT makes one rich.

The world works and toils for riches. We have them simply as a result of being in the family. God takes pleasure in our prosperity.[3] Because of Jesus' love for us He was actually made poor so that we could be made rich.[4] The Lord is good and His mercy endures forever. Prosperity and abundance come from a good God.

---

[2] Mark 10
[3] Psalm 35:27
[4] 2 Corinthians 8:9

Confession

Because of Jesus' love for me He became poor so I could be made rich.

11

ABUNDANCE IS GOOD

Genesis 12:2...I will bless you...and you shall be a blessing.

Let's continue with the thought that abundance is good. There are many reasons why God does not desire to give us just enough. Let me just share three of them. First of all, if He gave us just enough we would not have any seed to sow, therefore, Genesis 8:22 would cease. Secondly, He gives us more than enough so that we can sow into the gospel, spread the gospel and get a return. This in turn gives us more seed to sow, more return on our seed, more seed to sow and more return on our seed and you get the point. In the entire process the kingdom of God increases. It takes money to preach the gospel.

Another reason He wants to give us more than we need is so that we can sow into the lives of others. He told Abraham that He would bless him and make him a blessing. God knows what brings the greatest joy into our lives. It is in having something to give to be a blessing to others. This, my friend is also the goodness of God. He gives us abundance so that we can bless our children and the needy around us—so that we can act like Him and be good to others. He wants to give us abundance so we can be good to others as He has been good to us!

The highest level of prosperity is giving led by the Spirit of God and the love of God. The more I walk in the love of God the more I will desire to prosper to bring people into the kingdom of God and bless others. This in turn brings more praise to our God. No wonder Paul called the grace of giving an indescribable gift[1]. Yes, God is truly good. Abundance is good.

· ·

CONFESSION

I am blessed and I am a blessing. I am blessed to be a blessing.

· ·

---

1 2 Corinthians 9:15

12

MARRIAGE IS GOOD

Proverbs 18:22, Whoever finds a wife finds a good thing and obtains favor of the Lord.

There should be no confusion on this one. God created marriage since He stated that it was not good for man to be alone. So marriage is good. What is marriage? It is the union of two individuals (of different sexes, I might add) that have come together in the presence of God to commit themselves totally to one another for life. God then takes their commitment and unites their spirits making them one.

This is good. A lifetime commitment. So we can add that commitment is good. In this day of living together without any commitment to one another, we must remember that marriage is good and good for us because it was created by a God that is absolute good.

Marriage is also a picture of how much God loves us. A man is told in the Bible to love his wife as Christ loved us and gave Himself for us. Marriage points to the total giving of Jesus to us as a man is told to give himself for his wife. A wife submits as all of us submit to the Lord when we recognize His great love.

At times we take marriage and make it oppressive where its' major components are selfishness and self-centeredness. But this is not the picture of our Savior. We could say He has been the ideal husband—always loving us, doing good for us, even dying for us after we had turned our backs to Him. Yes, thank God for marriage, for giving us a vehicle to commit to one another. Can you imagine what condition society would be in without it? Someone rightly said once that marriage grows us up. It also provides glue for society.

So if today you are in a challenging marriage remember that our good God created it for your good. By faith begin to call it good. It is God's desire that your marriage become a channel for His goodness to flow into your life. Thank God for giving us marriage. He is a good God and His mercy endures forever.

Confession

I call my marriage good and good coming from it because my God who is good created it for my good.

13

FULL OF COMPASSION

Psalm 145:8, The Lord is gracious and full of compassion...

Matthew 14:14, And when Jesus went out He saw a great multitude; and He was moved with compassion for them, and healed their sick.

The Lord is full of compassion relates to the thoughts in chapter two on the Lord being absolute good. Meditate on this for a minute that the Lord is full of compassion. Not half or three-quarters full but completely full of compassion. He is full of compassion toward you and me. Therefore, His thoughts are never to steal, kill, or destroy but only to restore what has been stolen, give life, and bless. The thought that the Lord is full of compassion indicates that all that He does is compassion based. All His thoughts are compassion based thoughts. But what of the hand of the Lord on those who come against us?

His compassion moves Him to protect us because we are in covenant with Him.

But He is also compassionate toward the sinner. That is why He sent Jesus and why He continues to give the sinner time to repent. He does not take pleasure in any person being lost, going to hell or not coming to the knowledge of His compassion. He is full of compassion. That is what makes God, God. That is His essence, His nature. That is what He wants us to know about Him that He is full of compassion. Compassion is not a feeling. Compassion is a person—Jesus. Compassion is action. It is what moves God to do for others. It is love in action. Compassion is good.

Confession

The Lord is full of compassion. All His actions toward me are compassion based.

14

THE LORD IS GOOD TO ALL

Psalm 145:9, The Lord is good to all, and His tender mercies are over all His works.

The Lord is good to <u>all</u>. He is not good toward some and frustrates others. This may be difficult for some people to believe especially those that have gone through calamities, horrific accidents or the death of a child. But the Lord IS good to all. We believe this because it is in the Word of God. Well, where was God when the heartbreaking event occurred? Right where we left Him. He is good toward all means that He is always speaking to us how to avert a calamity but we have been too busy many times to be able to hear Him. It is never God's desire for harm to come to us.

A more appropriate question should be where is God NOW not where was He WHEN…? He is right there to give His comfort to all. 2 Corinthians 1:3 calls our Heavenly Father the Father of mercies and the God of all comfort. It goes on to state in the next verse that He comforts all. Where is God? Right next to you my friend, ready to comfort you if you are still grieving over a loss.

Believe the Word that He is full of compassion and the God of all comfort. Receive His compassion by simply telling Him that you believe His word and thanking Him. You may not understand all the reasons why something happened but His compassion will heal you. You can then hear clearly how to avert any further robberies by the devil. He loves you and His tender mercies are over you today. Believe and receive.

Now live expecting to see His goodness show up every day in your life. The Lord is good to all.

Confession

Thank you Heavenly Father for being the Father of mercies and the God of all comfort. I receive Your mercy and comfort today. Your tender mercies are over me today.

The God of Restoration, Part One

Joel 2:25, "So I will restore to you the years that the swarming locust has eaten,…

Because God is good He restores what the devil steals. God is the God of restoration. Look at the story of Job. Though not the cause of Job's losses, as many claim incorrectly, God restored double to Job what the devil stole from him. Just look at Job chapter 42:10 where the Word clearly states that the Lord restored Job's losses. Most people who believe that the Lord was behind Job's losses, since He supposedly gave the devil permission to attack Job, forget this verse. God is the restorer not the one who steals, kills or destroys[1].

Job himself stated[2] that the thing he had feared had come on him. Job's fear opened him up to be robbed.

---
1 John 10:10
2 Job 3:25

Later he realized where he had missed it. He repented and got back in faith. God restored his losses just like He restored the back wages to the Jewish nation when they left Egypt. That is the reason they left Egypt with silver and gold.[3] God will restore your losses as well because He is good and His mercy endures forever. He is not the taker. He is the restorer.

Begin to do what Isaiah 42:22 states and declare restoration to the things that the devil has stolen from you. Do not give up until the devil returns at least twice[4] and even seven times[5] what he stole. God is the God of restoration because He is good and His mercy endures forever.

Confession

My God is the God of restoration so today I declare restoration to all the things that the enemy has stolen from me.

---

[3] Psalm 105:37
[4] Isaiah 40:2
[5] Proverbs 6:30-31

16

THE GOD OF RESTORATION, PART TWO

Joel 2:25, So I will restore to you the years…

I want to continue with the God of restoration. I especially like the above noted phrase in Joel 2:25. God is a restorer of years. Think of this for a few minutes. Do you need any years restored? It is easier for many people to believe for things to be restored but what of years restored? What Is the Lord saying here?

Well think of this for a minute. When long term illness occurs years are stolen. Time we could have spent with our loved ones seems lost forever. God not only wants to heal but restore what the sick years stole from you and not just in terms of losses of wages and the like. He wants to bring your health back to where it was before you got sick AND MORE. However, He wants to also restore the <u>time</u> lost that you could not spend with your loved ones. Remember that He is the God of the MUCH MORE.

Look further at this point. Has your strength been stolen? He wants to return, to restore, the years stolen and give you your strength back to what it was years ago and MORE. He wants to restore the YEARS. You may have thought that you would never be able to do what you could do years ago but not so.

Can you see something here that most people have not believed God for? He wants to turn the clock back. Can He do it? Well review the story in 2 Kings chapter 20 verses 9 and 10. He turned the clock back then and He has not changed. Speak restoration to your body and let Him renew your youth like the eagles'.

Do you have loved ones that have wandered from the Lord? Remember that Jeremiah 31:15-17 states that God will bring them back. Speak restoration to your relationships and the years that seem lost will be restored. Never look back and say that the past years are lost forever. He is the God of restoration because He is good.

Confession

I declare restoration to my body in Jesus' name. I declare my youth renewed, restored like the eagles'. I declare my relationships restored, in Jesus' name. What has been stolen is being restored to me in all areas of my life.

17

TASTE AND SEE

Psalm 34:8, Oh, taste and see that the Lord is good;

The desire of God is that we taste that He is good and that His mercy endures forever. Before we discuss how we taste the goodness of the Lord let's think of the fact that God wants us to **know** that He is good. He yearns for all to know that He is good. Yes, He wants us to know that He is Omnipotent and All Knowing but more importantly that He is good. Actually, it is more important to have a revelation of His goodness than His great power or we will not believe that He wants to manifest His power on our behalf. Remember the leper who ran to Jesus and stated in Matthew chapter 8, "If you want to you can make me clean." He knew Jesus could (His power) but was not sure Jesus wanted to (His goodness).

So how do we taste? You taste by going to His Word, reading the scriptures on His goodness and believing them. Tasting means to have experiential knowledge. I can tell you how good a certain food tastes but until you believe what I am telling you and eat the food then you will never know. It is in the believing what I tell you and acting on what I state that you now know. You will never know the goodness of your Heavenly Father until you read the Bible, believe it and receive it.

Put your preconceived ideas about God aside and read scriptures on His goodness. Then declare every day, "The Lord is good and His mercy endures forever." Make a quality decision to never let your mouth declare anything but the goodness of God.[1] Before you know it you will be tasting and seeing His goodness. Actually it has been in our lives all this time but we are now believing it and becoming aware of it. Becoming aware of it causes it to manifest more in our lives since we will be expecting it more. Taste and see.

Confession

Every day I am tasting that the Lord is good.
He is good to me.

---

1 Psalm 145:3-9

18

HIS GOODNESS LEADS TO REPENTANCE

Romans 2:4 ... not knowing that the goodness of the Lord leads you to repentance?

We have not really believed this scripture in preaching to the lost. We have, by and large, preached about hell and how much God hates sin. In our quest to teach how much God hates sin we have forgotten to teach the world how much He loves sinners. Yes, our Father hates sin because it hurts our relationships and can open the door to the devil. He still loves us but sin does carry consequences. Sin will not destroy your righteousness but it can unravel your relationships.

What about people who have departed from the Lord? We usually try to beat them into repentance not believing for the goodness of God to lead them to repentance. Here is a good thing to pray—"Father I believe your goodness is leading my loved one to repentance. Manifest your goodness to them."

However, the above noted verse is not just for the sinner. As believers, we repent—we change our way of thinking (which is what repentance means) when we get a revelation of His love for us. Our major task as Christians once we get born-again is to begin the renewing of our mind. We take the Word of God and change our way of thinking to what the Word states. When we receive a revelation of His goodness our thinking changes about the way we think of God, our Father. This is undoubtedly the first area we need repentance in.

We will begin to think that He is for us[1] and is on our side.[2] On top of this, we will not look for a way to see how much sin we can get away with and still make it to heaven. We will desire it less and less as we understand how good He is. A revelation of His goodness and grace gives us victory over sin.[3]

Truly, His goodness leads you to repentance, to change, to think differently about Jesus, all He has done and provided for you and wants to do for you. Allow His goodness to lead you to repentance, to change your mind about God. He loves you.

---

1 Romans 8:31
2 Psalm 118:6
3 Romans 6:14

Confession

My thinking is changing every day because I have received a revelation of His love and goodness.

19

THE GOOD SHEPHERD

John 10:14, "I am the good shepherd; and I know My sheep, and am known by My own.

In one of his messages Keith Moore talks about a shepherd that has a reputation for being a good shepherd. He is not from your part of the country so when you hear of him coming to your town you want so much to see him and his flock. When he gets to your town you see him leading his sheep. He is well built and stately, and even smiles coming into town.

But then you see something that totally surprises you. You see the sheep behind him and many are maimed and some are bleeding. You can see the problem right away. They have not been cared for. Well you do not care what others have said about him or how stately he appears he is NOT a good shepherd.

Well, we DO have a good shepherd.[1] He loves us and takes good care of us. He has laid down His life for us. This makes Him THE good shepherd. He cares for us as noted in Psalm 23. Everything in this Psalm is a manifestation of His goodness as a shepherd.

Verse 1: He provides.

Verse 2: He gives rest.

Verse 3: He comforts and guides.

Verse 4: He delivers us from fear.

Verse 5: He brings us to His banqueting table and anoints us with His good Spirit.

The Psalm finishes with the statement that surely goodness and mercy shall follow me all the days of my life. Why? Because we have a good shepherd. Ultimately, the good shepherd is willing to lay down His life for the sheep. He did. He is truly good.

- -

Confession

> I have a good shepherd who takes good care of me.

- -

---

1 John 10:11

20

THE GOSPEL

Romans 1:16, For I am not ashamed of the gospel of Christ,…

The word gospel means good news. Many people incorrectly see the gospel as the bad news. But Christianity is not a long list of what you can't do if you want to become a Christian. It is not even a list of things that you can't do once you become one. Furthermore, the gospel is not telling sinners that hell awaits them if they do not repent. This statement is correct but not the gospel.

No, the good news of the Gospel is that He loves you and is good. He took the sin of all mankind and is not holding our sins against us.[1] Not only did He take all our sin and judgment on the cross but gave us His right standing with the Father.[2] He has sent us out as ministers

---

1 2 Corinthians 5:19
2 2 Corinthians 5:21

of reconciliation to tell the world that God is not holding their sins against them.

God is not angry at mankind since all His anger was placed on Jesus when He took our place. God's justice has been satisfied. All our sins, past, present and future sins have been paid for.[3] Remember that the angels proclaimed peace on earth goodwill TOWARD men when they announced the birth of Jesus. God's goodwill, His favor, as another translation states, has come. The gospel is the grace of God—His unmerited undeserved favor toward men.

Look at it this way. The gospel is God doing us a favor. A favor! He came and paid the debt we could not pay. This is the gospel of the grace of God![4] Now that we have received Him He wants to do us favors every day! What a gospel—what good news. The Lord is truly good.

· ·

Confession

I am not ashamed of the gospel of Christ,
the gospel of the grace of God. God has
forgiven me of all my sins, past, present and
future. His Grace, His favor is mine today.
God is doing me favors every day.

· ·

---

3 Colossians 2:13
4 Galatians 1:6

21

GOD THE GREAT

Psalm 145:3,7, Great is the Lord, and greatly to be praised; They shall utter the memory of Your great goodness,…

Nehemiah 9:32, "Now therefore, our God, The great, the mighty, and awesome God, Who keeps covenant and mercy:…

God is great because He is good. Most of the time when we think of great men or women we don't usually associate them with the word good. We are not saying they were bad, of course. However, what we usually think about is their great feats. Take, for example, Alexander the Great. We call men (or women) like him great because of monumental feats such as conquering great armies. But were they truly great?

Maybe it is time we reevaluate what great is. A person is great not just because of his or her accomplishments or great feats but because of the good they were able to do for others. Their life and ways have blessed others. The goals in their lives were not necessarily to become great but to do good—to bless others. In their desire to do good to others they became great.

In Psalm 145 we see:

Verse 3: that God is great and that His greatness is unsearchable,

Verse 4: that His acts are mighty,

Verse 5: wondrous

Verse 6: and awesome.

Verse 7: At the end of all this, the psalmist mentions the great goodness of God.

So let's summarize that God is great, mighty, wondrous, and awesome because He is good—because of His great goodness. God is Great because He is good.

Confession

I declare great, mighty, wondrous, and awesome things coming to my life today because the Lord is great in goodness toward me.

22

RELEASING HIS GOODNESS IN OUR LIVES, PART ONE

Psalm 118:1, Oh, give thanks to the Lord, for He is good! For His mercy endures forever.

Psalm 66:12 (Amplified) ...You brought us into a broad, moist place [to abundance and refreshment and the open air].

In meditating this verse recently I began to see a mighty way to release His goodness and mercy into our lives—simply by thanking Him that He is good and that His mercy endures forever. Simple isn't it? We have heard much about the power of praise. We need to hear even more. God inhabits the praises of His people.

In the next few verses in Psalm 118 the Lord commands us to SAY that His mercy endures forever. Let me quote the Psalm.

Verse 2, Let Israel now say, "His mercy endures forever."

Verse 3, Let the house of Aaron now say, "His mercy endures forever."

Verse 4, Let those who fear the Lord now say, "His mercy endures forever."

In verse 5 of the same Psalm, the psalmist adds that he called on the Lord and the Lord set him in a broad place. Do you see the connection? His praise caused the release of God's goodness and mercy into his life.

No, we are not just praising Him to get God to work on our behalf. We could say that the praise of God not so much moves Him as it moves us to focus away from whatever test we may be experiencing and instead focus on His goodness. In praise we stay in faith. We praise Him because He IS good and His mercy does endure forever. He is worthy of our praise. Then get ready for Him to set you in a place that is broad, moist, abundant and refreshing. Yes, the Lord truly is good!

Confession

I declare that God has set me in a broad, moist, abundant and refreshing place because He is good and His mercy endures forever.

23

RELEASING HIS GOODNESS IN OUR LIVES, PART TWO

Psalm 92:1, It is a good thing to give thanks to the Lord,...

Let's continue with releasing the goodness of God into our lives. Psalm 92:1 states that it is a good thing to give thanks to the Lord. A good thing indeed because He is good and inhabits the praises of His people. 2 Chronicles 6:41 tells us that we are to rejoice in His goodness. So where does this leave feeling sorry for ourselves? Outside, of course.

To continue with 2 Chronicles 6:41, the saints (that is you and me my brethren) are told to rejoice in His goodness. This shows us that the saints are to have the distinguishing mark of joy. We do not let the economy or whatever get us down. When negative circumstances come we rejoice. We do not rejoice that they come but that we are victorious over them because we trust in the goodness of our Heavenly Father.

We can return to Psalm 27:13 which states, "I would have lost heart, unless I had believed that I would see the goodness of the Lord in the land of the living." We should not faint and we will not faint (lose heart) if we continually trust in His goodness. Release it into your life by casting all your cares on Him,[1] opening your mouth and praising Him that He is good. 1 Peter 5:7 in the Amplified version states that we should cast all our cares on Him because He cares for us affectionately and watchfully. This is something we need to have a revelation of. This undoubtedly was what the Psalmist of old was thinking about when he talked of the tender mercies of the Lord.[2]

Keep your mind on Him by praising Him. His promise is that as we do so He will keep us in perfect peace.[3] It truly is a good thing to give Him thanks.

---

[1] 2 Peter 5:7
[2] Psalm 145:9
[3] Isaiah 26:3

Confession

I do not faint because I live in expectancy of seeing the goodness of the Lord in my life. I rejoice in His goodness.

24

A Year Crowned with Goodness

Psalm 65:11, You crown the year with your goodness...

A year crowned with goodness. Wow! Most people just want to have a good day. A good week is beyond the mindset of almost all people. But a YEAR crowned with goodness is truly exceedingly abundantly above all we can ask or think.[1] But this is the will of God to do beyond what we in the natural can ask or think.

Think for minute. What would a year crowned with goodness be like? Goodness showing up every day. Unexpected blessings every week. Surprises every time we turn around. 'Suddenlies' to use the word coined by others. Malachi 3:10 showing up where we just do not have room for all the blessings. On top of this, being able and having the resources to do all He calls us to do. 2 Corinthians 9:8

---

1 Ephesians 3:20

states, "that you always having all sufficiency in all things may have abundance for every good work." Always having for our needs AND always having to bless those works and people God places it in our hearts to bless. What a way to live.

Yes, Brother Samuel, we will live like this in heaven. No, Psalm 65 was written to people on the earth. Maybe you just can't believe in such a year. However, a year crowned with goodness is possible because it is in the Word of God and His Word is His will. Luke 4:19 (Amplified Version) clearly states that Jesus came to "proclaim the day when…the free favors of God profusely abound."

Begin to confess this—"My year is crowned with His goodness." God desires a year crowned with goodness for His people. Reject sin consciousness and embrace God's grace. Regardless of whatever occurs this year keep saying it and expecting a year crowned with goodness because God is good and His mercy endures forever.

Confession

My year is crowned with goodness—
with God Himself.

25

THE CROWN OF GOODNESS

Psalm 8:5, ... (You) have crowned him (man) with glory and honor...

Now let's deal with the word crown. As we stated in the last chapter, the Lord wants to crown our year with His goodness. Don't think of a small crown on your head. This is not what the word means. This word really means encircled for protection, to compass about. God has encircled us with His goodness. We are encompassed about with His goodness. We can say that crowned is to be overtaken with the blessings of God.

This sounds to me like what God did with Job. The complaint that the devil had with God was that He had placed a hedge around Job. This was actually the Blessing wall. This is what crowns us with His goodness. The crown of His goodness is the Blessing wall—the Blessings of the Lord that makes us rich (Proverbs 10:22). This is the same Blessing that God declared over Adam in

Genesis 1:28 when He empowered him to BE fruitful, multiply, replenish, subdue and have dominion. When it is operating in our lives we live in an impenetrable realm. We have already seen that to be crowned is to be encircled for protection.

Now let us stay within the Blessing wall, the crown, the encirclement. Stay in love. Stay in faith and stay under the crown. As you continue to believe in His goodness you stay under the crown. How simple can this be? You are crowned with goodness because the Lord is good and His mercy endures forever.

Confession

I am encompassed about with His goodness.
I am encompassed about with THE Blessing
of the Lord and crowned with glory,
honor and His goodness.

26

GOODNESS AND MERCY ARE FOLLOWING ME

Psalm 23:6, Surely goodness and mercy shall follow me all the days of my life; and I will dwell in the house of the Lord forever.

Have you ever felt that evil was following you; that everywhere you turned something negative was happening? God does not want us living this way. It was Job who stated that the evil he feared had come to him. I remember once talking to a family member who when I asked how they were told me directly, "one bad thing after another bad thing." I told them why not begin to declare one good thing after another good thing. That was the confession of faith of King David who wrote Psalm 23. Frankly, we cannot say that everything was always perfect in his life but he decided to make his confession of faith anyway. Have you ever realized that Psalm 23 is one faith confession after another?

Say it. Surely goodness and mercy are following me today and every day of my life. In Psalm 144:2 (KJV) the psalmist calls the Lord God his (the psalmist's) goodness. Can you see this? Goodness is not a thing. Goods are things but the goodness we are studying is a person. Get this. The psalmist in Psalm 23:6 was literally saying surely <u>God</u> is following me all the days of my life. Wow! How can we not overcome every obstacle coming into our lives when goodness and mercy Himself is following us all the days of our lives!

Confession

Surely goodness and mercy are following me today and every day of my life. Goodness Himself is following me all the days of my life!

27

IN THE BEGINNING, GOOD

Genesis 1:1, In the beginning God created the heavens and the earth.

If goodness is a person then we can now see even more why everything God created when He formed the heavens and the earth was good. A good God can only create good. Perhaps you have never meditated on this at length that everything, everything, everything God created was good and beneficial for the man and woman He was about to create. From this we see further evidence that the nature of God is good and that what He will do for us for all eternity will be good. In other words, if in the beginning good, then for all eternity, good!

Let me give some synonyms of the word good (Hebrew, tôwb) as used in the creation story—best, better, beautiful, bountiful, joyful, sweet and precious. As we have already mentioned, the word also means prosperity and wealth. In creation we see God's will for all men for all time. In the creation story even the gold was mentioned as being good. And yet, when He created man the scriptures state He called His creation "very good."

Let me say it again. Good is God's will for all men for all time. If it was in the garden it was good. If it was not there it was not and never will be good. Let's keep it simple. Good is His will because He is good and good is what was seen in the garden. God's will was never plan 'B'. Plan 'A' was good for all men for all time. When man fell He came to restore plan 'A' because He is good.

Confession

Because God is good I declare that best, better, beautiful, joyful, sweet and precious things are coming to my life from Him today.

28

HIS GLORY

Exodus 33:18, And he said, "Please, show me your glory."

Exodus 33:19, Then He said, "I will make all my goodness pass before you,…

John 17:22, "And the glory which you gave me I have given them, that they may be one just as We are one:

Exodus chapters 33 and 34 have one of the greatest Bible stories. Moses in the above noted scriptures asked God to show him His glory. God responded by telling Moses that he was going to see His goodness.[1] In Exodus 34:6 after God had told Moses that he could only see His back, the Lord passes by and proclaims, "The Lord, the Lord God merciful and gracious, longsuffering, and abundant in goodness and truth." So we can see that God's glory is His goodness—His abundant goodness.

---

1 Exodus 33:19

1 Thessalonians 2:12 states that God has called us into His kingdom and glory. 2 Peter 1:3 shows us that God has called us by glory and virtue. In 1 Peter 5:10 we see that God has called us to His eternal glory. Finally, 2 Thessalonians 2:14 states that God has called us to the obtaining of the glory of our Lord Jesus Christ.

There is a glory reserved only for our Lord. However, He has called us to sit with Him in heavenly places[2] at the right hand of the Father and share and participate in His glory. What should be our response? Well to sit down, enjoy the glory and give Him the glory. Do not sit outside and call yourself unworthy. We were unworthy but He still came to bring us to glory.[3] He is good and His mercy endures forever.

••••••••••••••••••••••••••••••••••••••

Confession

I have been called into His kingdom and glory—to sit with Jesus in heavenly places because the Lord is good and His mercy endures forever.

••••••••••••••••••••••••••••••••••••••

---

2 Ephesians 2:6
3 Hebrews 2:10

29

THE GOOD HAND OF THE LORD

Ezra 7:9... and on the first day of the fifth month he came to Jerusalem, according to the good hand of his God upon him.

Ezra 7:9 describes the "...good hand of his God upon him." He uses the same phrase in 8:18. Then in Nehemiah 2:18, Nehemiah comments on the hand of God which was good upon him.

This phrase 'the hand of the Lord' always refers to blessing, honor and favor when the hand of the Lord is upon His people. When the hand of the Lord is stretched out against the adversaries of His people the phrase always refers to judgment.

Observe the disciples praying in Acts 4:29-30. They prayed, "Now, Lord, look on their threats, and grant to Your servants that with all boldness they may speak Your word, by stretching out Your hand to heal, and that signs and wonders may be done through the name of Your holy Servant Jesus." A few verses later we read that with great power the apostles gave witness to the resurrection of the Lord Jesus and that great grace was upon them. So the hand of the Lord produced signs and wonders.

The hand of the Lord is His grace and His favor. It can also refer to the Blessing and to His goodness. Believe that it is upon you to help you do what in the natural you cannot do. Then He will get all the glory. It is upon you today. Thank Him for it.

Confession

The good hand of the Lord, His favor, grace,
empowerment, blessing and honor
is upon me today.

30

FILLED WITH ALL GOODNESS

Romans 15:14, Now I myself am confident concerning you, my brethren, that you also are full of goodness...

The apostle makes a tremendous statement when he called the Romans full of goodness. Have you ever met someone that you considered FULL of goodness? Perhaps you feel that there are not many Christians like that around. But consider this. If goodness is a person[1] and He has come in His fullness to live inside of us are we not filled with all goodness? Yes we are. The commission of the believer is now to go and do the works of Jesus, to act like Him. Dare I say to be good like Him? Of course, not in ourselves but partaking of His goodness which is His nature.

---

1 Page 71, Chapter 26

We need to stop seeing ourselves as "sinners saved by grace." We were sinners, got saved by grace and are now present tense, today, right now, and not when we get to heaven, filled with all goodness. The more we recognize that we are spirit beings and that our spirits are perfect and filled with all goodness, the more we can do the works, the good works Jesus did.

Most Christians identify themselves with their body but we are not our bodies. Of course, we need to present our bodies to God as living sacrifices and renew our minds. However, our <u>spirits</u> are recreated in the image of God and filled with all that God is. If this is not the goodness of God toward His children then what is it? He is truly good.

CONFESSION

I have been filled with all goodness,
with God Himself.

SHOW AND TELL

John 14:12… I say to you, he that believes in Me, the works that I do shall he do also;

In a previous book (Amazing Love) I mentioned how the Lord shared with me the thought to treat others like the Lord is good and His mercy endures forever. He impressed on me that after discovering and receiving that the Lord is good and His mercy endures forever the next step is to treat others like the Lord is good and His mercy endures forever. Our commission as Christians is now to go out and do good. Not to be saved or be right with God but because we want others to know His goodness. The Lord needs us telling others of His goodness and demonstrating His goodness to others.

Ephesians 2:10 states that we were created to do good works. Hebrews 13:16 mentions that we must not forget to do good and that with such sacrifices God is well pleased. A favorite of mine is 1 Peter 3:13 that states in the Amplified version of the Bible to be zealous followers of that which is good. I could go on and on but the major question is what is a good action? You already know this answer since you have read this book.

Acts 10:38 states that Jesus went about doing good and healing all that were oppressed. Good is what Jesus did and does. As noted above Jesus stated that the works He did we can do and greater. Good is anything Jesus did in the Scriptures. Remember Jesus stated that He only did what He saw His Father do and only said what He heard His Father say. These are the guidelines. If Jesus did it in the Bible it is good. He healed the sick. He helped the poor. He loved children. I can go on and on. Read THE Book and imitate the Master. Go out and do good and tell others that He is a good God and loves them.

Paul indicated in Romans 2:4 that the goodness of God leads people to repentance. Let's show people the goodness of God. Others will not know the goodness of God except through us. Show and tell.

CONFESSION

I treat others like the Lord is good and His mercy endures forever. The good works Jesus did I can do also.

Epilogue

Receive Him Who Is Goodness— Come on Home

My reader, I trust that by now you have a greater revelation of the goodness of the God of the Bible. If you have never invited Him into your heart why not do it now? He paid all the debt we could not pay to bring us back to the Garden of Eden and more. He wants to come in but waits for your invitation. Just pray this simple prayer:

> "Lord Jesus I believe You died for me and were raised from the dead. I now invite You into my life to be my Lord and Saviour. Teach me more every day about Your great love and goodness. Amen."

You are now back home. You are now born-again. Write us if you need a Bible or to find a church near you. I Bless you in Jesus name! Now tell others that God has been good to you!

Verses on the Goodness of God

Ezra 8:22,…Because we had spoken to the king, saying, "The hand of our God is upon all those for good who seek Him…"

Nehemiah 9:25, And they took strong cities and a rich land…And delighted themselves in Your great goodness.

Psalm 118:1, Oh, give thanks to the Lord, for He is good! For His mercy endures forever.

Psalm 107:8, Oh, that men would give thanks to the Lord for His goodness,…

Exodus 34:6, And the Lord passed before him and proclaimed, "The Lord, the Lord God, merciful and gracious, longsuffering, and abounding in goodness and truth,

Matthew 7:11, If you then, being evil, know how to give good gifts to your children, how much more will your Father who is in heaven give good things to those who ask Him!

Psalm 84:11, No good thing will He withhold from those that walk uprightly.

Psalm 92:1, It is good to give thanks to the Lord, And to sing praises to Your name, O Most High;

Psalm 145:7, They shall utter the memory of Your great goodness,...

Psalm 145:8-9, The Lord is gracious and full of compassion, Slow to anger and great in mercy. The Lord is good to all, And His tender mercies are over all His works.

Titus 2:14, Who gave Himself for us,...(to) purify for Himself His own special people, zealous for good works.

Appendix

Amazing Love Ministries

Amazing Love Ministries (formerly Christian Faith Center) was established in 2001. We are a non denominational and bilingual church, part of the FCF fellowship of churches.

Our pastor's life changed in 1975 when as a young man he discovered John 14:12, indicating that the age of miracles and signs and wonders had never ceased.

Our vision is to proclaim the love and the goodness of God to a lost and dying world and equip the saints to do the works of Jesus.

Pastor Samuel Martinez was ordained in 1986. He teaches with humor and clarity the love of God, who we are in Christ Jesus and our authority as believers.

All contact information is listed here:

Email: Smartinez@cfaith.com

Correspondence:
Amazing Love Ministries
216 S. Citrus
P O Box 503
West Covina, CA 91791

About the Author

Samuel Martinez was ordained in 1986 and has been a full-time pastor since 2001. Prior to his work in the ministry, he served in the counseling field, with a master's degree in Marriage, Family and Child Counseling. Pastor Martinez's church offers both English and Spanish services, and his favorite themes to teach include the love and goodness of God. Pastor Martinez and his wife have been married over 45 years.

www.ingramcontent.com/pod-product-compliance
Lightning Source LLC
Chambersburg PA
CBHW071533080526
44588CB00011B/1661